Chapel Springs

COOKBOOK

by Ane Mulligan

Ashley,
Your encouragement
and love for my stories
has meant the world to me.

Lighthouse Publishing
of the Carolinas

CHAPEL SPRINGS COOKBOOK BY ANE MULLIGAN
Published by Lighthouse Publishing of the Carolinas
2333 Barton Oaks Dr., Raleigh, NC, 27614

ISBN: 978-1-941103-34-0
Copyright © 2015 by Ane Mulligan
Cover design by Ken Raney: www.kenraney.com
Interior design by Karthick Srinivasan

Available in print from your local bookstore, online, or from the publisher
at: www.lighthousepublishingofthecarolinas.com

For more information on this book and the author visit: www.anemulligan.com

Brought to you by the creative team at LighthousePublishingoftheCarolinas.com:
Eva Marie Everson, Rowena Kuo, Barb King, Michelle Creech, Brian Cross, and Eddie Jones.

Library of Congress Cataloging-in-Publication Data
Mulligan, Ane
Chapel Springs Cookbook / Ane Mulligan 1st ed.

Printed in the United States of America

INTRODUCTION

Introduction

It is my great pleasure to welcome y'all to this official collection of recipes from some of Chapel Springs' best cooks. There are even a few recipes from me, since in addition to my tireless work of serving the residents of our fair town, I do happen to be a pretty fair chef. I heartily recommend Felix's Classic Firehouse Chili.

I'm not sure what all is in here, but I'm hoping to find more than a couple of Dee Lindstrom's finest confections. Dee is the owner of *Dee's 'n' Doughs*, our local bakery. And I suspect Eileen Carlson, a lovely antique, er, the owner of our lovely antique shop, will have a treat or two for you. Her treats always make me smile.

Of course, we'll all be glad to find the recipes for some of Patsy Kowalski's and Joel Bennett's grandest creations. Be sure to look for Beethoven's Beans. I swear at any town pitch-in, if you're not first in line you won't get any! Fortunately, being mayor, I am always first in line.

So, welcome to Chapel Springs! Sit for a spell and have a glass of sweet tea and a pastry. If you haven't visited town yet, I invite you to do so at your earliest convenience. After all, it's all spruced up nice now, thanks to yours truly—and our many generous volunteers!

One final word. Call it a warning—and one you should be thankful to receive! If you see a recipe with the name "Claire Bennett" on it, just turn the page fast and pretend you never saw it. Trust me on this. As the mayor, would I lie to you?

Felix Riley, Mayor of Chapel Springs

Table of Contents

BREAKFAST

Slow Cooker Sausage Breakfast Casserole

The Official Breakfast of Chapel Springs,
From Mayor Felix Riley*

(As mayor I have long debated with myself about whether I could declare this the official breakfast of Chapel Springs. And I've decided I can. So, enjoy the official Chapel Springs Breakfast Casserole.)

INGREDIENTS

1 pkg.	(26-32 ounces) frozen shredded hash brown potatoes
1 pkg.	Jimmy Dean® Hearty Original Sausage Crumbles
2 C	(8 ounces) shredded mozzarella cheese
½ C	(2 ounces) shredded Parmesan cheese
½ C	julienne cut sun dried tomatoes packed in oil, drained
6	green onions, sliced
12	eggs
½ C	milk
½ tsp	salt
¼ tsp	ground black pepper

METHOD

1. Spray a 6 quart slow cooker with cooking spray. Layer half the potatoes on the bottom of slow cooker.

2. Top with half of the sausage, mozzarella and parmesan cheese, sun dried tomatoes and green onion. Repeat steps 1 and 2 until all are used.

3. Beat eggs, milk, salt and pepper in large bowl with a wire whisk until well blended.

4. Pour evenly over potato-sausage mixture.

5. Cook on low setting for 8 hours or on high setting for 4 hours or until eggs are set.

NOTES:

Substitute 1 C chopped fresh tomato for sun dried tomatoes, if desired.

Substitute 1 pkg. regular flavor Jimmy Dean* Pork Sausage Roll, cooked, crumbled for Jimmy Dean* Hearty Original Sausage Crumbles.

I have been known to add bacon, just for kicks. How much? All I can say is, "enough." Whatever that means for you. Just layer it in with the sausage.

*Mayor Felix Riley is Claire Bennett's nemesis. They butt heads on nearly every detail in Chapel Springs. You'll want to read the books, if you haven't already, to see their next escapade.

Dee's Dough Nut Bites

From Dee Lindstrom of *Dee's 'n' Doughs* fame
Taught my kids to bake with these

INGREDIENTS

1	Can of jumbo biscuits
	Vegetable oil of your choice
½ C	sugar

(you can also use, frozen bread dough
THAWED... NOT frozen)

Cut your biscuit dough into 1/4 inch pieces. (thawed
bread dough - cut bite sized)

METHOD

(Warning to Claire - frozen dough can cause oil to overflow or CATCH ON FIRE)

1. Use enough oil to make 1 to 2 inches of oil in a
    heavy duty pan (preferably a cast iron skillet). You
    could us a FryDaddy if available.

2. Drop Dough Nut Bites into the oil, a few at a time.
    watch them, they cook really fast, probably less
    than 1 minute. You might want to flip them.

3. Take them out when they get lightly browned on both sides. Set your fried dough on a paper towel for a minute or two, then roll them in sugar, or with Cinnamon added into the sugar. You can also make a glaze to dip them in by mixing Confectioners sugar and small amount of milk.

** Vegetable oil Directions: (Now Claire, please pay attention here...) Let the oil get REALLY hot; if it's not hot enough, it will make your Dough Nut Bites greasy. If it's too hot, it could catch FIRE!

Fruity Baked Oatmeal

From Ellie Grant, Chapel Springs Librarian*

Serves 9

INGREDIENTS

3 C	quick-cooking oats
I C	packed brown sugar
2 tsp	baking powder
I tsp	salt
½ tsp	ground cinnamon
2 eggs,	lightly beaten
I C	fat-free milk
½ C	butter, melted
¾ C	chopped peeled tart apple
1/3 C	chopped fresh or frozen peaches
1/3 C	fresh or frozen blueberries

Additional fat-free milk, optional

METHOD

1. In a large bowl, combine the oats, brown sugar, baking powder, salt and cinnamon.

2. Combine the eggs, milk and butter, then add to the dry ingredients. Stir in apple, peaches, and blueberries.

3. Pour into an 8-in. square baking dish coated with nonstick cooking spray.

4. Bake uncovered at 350° F for 35-40 minutes or until a knife inserted near the center comes out clean. Cut into squares. Serve with milk if desired.

*Poor Ellie is under her mama's thumb. A middle child, Ellie's sisters fled Chapel Springs, leaving her to take care of their ailing mama. Ellie's fiancé got tired of waiting and married somebody else. The years have passed and Ellie became the town's spinster. But lately she and Happy Drayton have been observed flirting with one another. And Happy loves oatmeal.

Twisted pretzel biscuit

From Hannah Tucker, Works as the Spa's receptionist

A easy kid friendly recipe that even Claire could make

INGREDIENTS

¼ C	melted butter
½ C	sugar and 1 ½ Tbsp cinnamon, mixed together in bowl
1	can refrigerator biscuits

METHOD

1. Can cut biscuits in half for smaller pretzels.

2. Roll out like play dough and twist into pretzel shape. Coat with melted butter and coat with cinnamon sugar mixture.

3. Place on ungreased cookie sheet and bake in oven at 350° until done about 8-15min.

APPETIZERS

Asparagus Tart

From Dee Lindstrom, Owner of Dee's 'n' Doughs*

INGREDIENTS

1	sheet frozen puff pastry, thawed
1/3 C	sour cream (or crème fraiche)
1 C	Gruyère cheese, shredded
1 lb	asparagus
1 Tbls	olive oil
	salt and pepper
	all-purpose flour, for work surface

METHOD

Preheat oven to 400°F.

1. Roll the puff pastry out on a floured surface, to a 16"x10" rectangle. Trim uneven edges. Place pastry on a baking sheet.

2. Lightly score pastry dough with a sharp knife 1" in from the edges to mark a rectangle. Pierce dough using a fork, inside the markings at 1/2-inch intervals. Bake 10 minutes.

3. Cool pastry slightly and brush inside border with crème fraiche (or sour cream), and sprinkle with cheese.

4. Trim the bottoms of the asparagus spears to fit crosswise inside the pastry. Alternating ends and tips, arrange in a single layer over cheese.

5. Drizzle with oil; season with salt and pepper. Bake 10-12 minutes or until spears are tender. Cut into squares and serve.

*Dee added these Asparagus Tarts as a lunch item or for an appetizer. Claire loves them, but then Dee made anything is Claire's favorite.

Bean, Corn & Tomato Salsa

From Morgan Smith, Manager of Chapel
Springs Spa*

INGREDIENTS

3 Tbls	lime juice
2 Tbls	olive oil
1	15 oz can Black beans, rinsed & drained
1	can corn kernels, drained
1	can diced tomatoes
¼ C	onion, finely chopped (I use sweet onions)
2 tsp	basil, minced
	salt & pepper to taste, and optional cayenne pepper to taste

METHOD

1. Mix all together and let stand 45 minutes, stirring once or twice.

2. Serve with tortilla chips

*And she's Lydia's daughter

Herb Cheese Stuffed Potatoes

From Chef Thornton*

INGREDIENTS

| | 2" round oblong red potato per person |

Herb & garlic cheese spread, recipe below

Grape tomatoes, cut in half (1/2 per potato half)

METHOD

1. Day before: cut the ends off the oblong red potatoes, then cut each in half at the widest point, so you have little round crowns.

2. Toss cut rounds in olive oil and place the largest cut side down on parchment lined baking sheet. Bake at 350° till golden, approx 20 minutes.

Chill on baking sheet, uncovered till next day.

Herb & garlic cheese:

1 lb	cream cheese, softened
¼ lb	salted butter
1 tsp	fresh ground cracked pepper
1 tsp	salt
1 Tbsp	fresh rosemary, finely minced

| ¼ C | finely minced green onion |
| I Tbsp | finely minced roasted garlic (add more to taste as one can never get too much garlic) |

Blend the softened cream cheese and all other ingredients and mix well. Cover and refrigerate for 24 hours, then bring to room temp before building potatoes.

To build, using a melon baller, core out center of the larger side of each potato round, then fill with herb cheese and crown with a half grape tomato.

*Chef Thornton was committed to Sunny Farms, where he plants herbs that are sold to anyone who doesn't live within 100 miles of Chapel Springs.

Smoked Gouda/Tuna/Melt Dip

From Chef Thornton*

INGREDIENTS

8	oz smoked Gouda, shredded (hold a bit back for topping)
8	oz cream cheese, softened
3	5-oz cans of tuna, drained
I Tbls	cracked ground peppercorn
I/3 C	mayonnaise

METHOD

1. Soften cream cheese and mix with the shredded Gouda until fully incorporated. Add the mayonnaise and pepper. Fold in the tuna.

2. Put into a baking dish and cover. Bake at 350° for 20 minutes.

3. Uncover, top with more Gouda and bake uncovered for 10 more minutes or until golden brown. Serve with crusty bread or crackers.

*After 3 months at Sunny Farms, Chef Thornton was allowed in the kitchen to cook for the other patients. As long as no one else enters the kitchen, he's fine and the twitch remains a thing of the past.

Southwest Corn Salsa

From Lydia Smith, Owner of Chapel Springs Spa*

INGREDIENTS

1 15 oz	can whole kernel corn, drained.
1 15 oz	can white Shoepeg corn, drained
1 C	chopped tomatoes
2	avocados, diced
½ C	purple onion diced
1	12 oz bottle green taco sauce
	Juice from 1 lime
1	large jalapeno, finely diced

METHOD

1. Combine all ingredients in a bowl and serve. If making ahead of time, wait until serving time to add avocado. Can be served with chips or crackers.

*Lydia Smith was a widow. She bought an old house up on a hill when she moved to Chapel Springs to be near her daughter, Morgan, and her sister, Lacey. People in Chapel Springs began calling her "the widow on the hill".

Texas Caviar

From Lydia Smith, Owner of Chapel Springs Spa

INGREDIENTS

1/3 C	chopped green onions
1	small can chopped green chilies
2 Tbsp	Vinegar
2	Jalapenos chopped
1 Tbsp	cilantro
1 tsp	olive oil
½ tsp	garlic salt
1 tsp	salt
½ tsp	onion salt
¼ tsp	cayenne pepper
½ C	tomatoes
1	can blackeyed peas, drained
1	can Shoepeg corn, drained
1	can whole kernel corn, drained
	Cilantro for garnish

METHOD

1. Combine all ingredients in a large bowl and gently toss. Cover and refrigerate. The longer it is refrigerated the better it is. Top with cilantro just before serving.

2. Serve with crackers or toast points.

SALADS

Avocado Potato Salad

By JoAnn Hanson, Pastor Seth's wife*

INGREDIENTS

6	medium red potatoes, unpeeled, cut in 1" cubes
2	avocados, peeled, pitted & cubed
2 Tbsp	fresh limejuice
½ C	chopped sweet onion
¼ C	fresh cilantro leaves, chopped

DRESSING

¼ C	fresh limejuice	2		cloves crushed garlic
2 Tbsp	honey mustard	2 tsp		sugar
1 tsp	salt	1 tsp		pepper
1 Tbsp	olive oil	½ C		plain nonfat yogurt

METHOD

1. Boil diced potatoes in large pot until just tender. While potatoes boil, cube avocados and toss with 2 Tbsp lime juice; set aside.

2. Drain potatoes and place in bowl of cold water. When potatoes are cool, drain well and place in large salad bowl.

3. Dressing: Whisk limejuice, garlic, mustard, sugar, salt, pepper, olive oil and yogurt in a medium bowl. Taste dressing and adjust seasonings. Pour dressing

over potatoes and toss. Gently fold in avocado, onion and cilantro.

4. Serve at room temperature, or cover tightly with plastic wrap and chill until serving (can be prepared up to 3 hours in advance).

5. Makes 8 – 1 cup servings.

*JoAnn is one of the "flower gals"

Broccoli Salad

From Cooper Benson

INGREDIENTS

2	heads broccoli, chopped
½ C	shredded cheese
I C	mayo
½ C	raisins or cranberry
½ C	sunflower seeds
	Bacon or bacon bits to taste
	carrots or cabbage slaw as desired
	You can add grapes, strawberry or spinach also.

METHOD

1. Mix well, refrigerate for 30 minutes.

Cooper Benson is Patsy's mama. She has a strange habit of counting the flatware.

Cole Slaw

From Patsy Kowalski

Serves 8

INGREDIENTS

I	med onion, chopped
I C	sugar
I C	vegetable oil
½ C	cider vinegar
1/3 C	mayonnaise
I tsp	salt
½ tsp	celery seed
I	med green cabbage, cored and shredded

METHOD

1. In a med bowl, combine the onion and sugar. Let it stand for 30 minutes. In a separate bowl, combine the oil, vinegar, mayonnaise, salt, and celery seed. Add this to the onion and sugar mix.

2. Pour this into a jar with a tight fitting lid. Shake to blend the dressing. Mix dressing with cabbage and enjoy. Don't overdress the cabbage.

Corn & Spinach Salad

By Leanna Wallace*

Serves 8

INGREDIENTS

½ C	chopped walnuts
I T	sugar
I ½ tsp	cider vinegar
I	6 oz pkg fresh baby spinach
I	med red bell pepper, diced
½	med sweet onion, diced
I C	frozen corn, thawed
I C	crumbled goat cheese
¼ C	Craisins

DRESSING:

3 T	cider vinegar
2 T	orange marmalade
2 T	mayonnaise
½ tsp	salt
½ tsp	pepper
¼ tsp	Worcestershire sauce

METHOD

1. In a heavy skillet, cook walnuts over medium heat until toasted, 3-4 minutes. Sprinkle with sugar and vinegar. Cook and stir an additional 2-4 minutes,

or until sugar is melted. Spread out on some foil to cool.

2. In a bowl, combine the spinach, red pepper, onion, corn, cheese and craisins. Add in the walnuts.

3. In a small bowl, whisk together the ingredients for the dressing, then pour over salad and toss.

*Leanna Wallace hasn't made her debut yet, but will in May of 2016 in *Home to Chapel Springs.*

Easy Livin' Salad

From Leanna Wallace

Serves 6

INGREDIENTS

1	(8 oz) pkg. Chicken flavored Rice-A-Roni cooked & chilled
2 C	Cooked chicken, diced
1	(3 oz) pkg. Dry salami, diced
3	Tomatoes, diced
1	Onion, diced
1 C	Chopped fresh parsley
3	Avocados, halved, pitted, and peeled

DRESSING

1 C	Vegetable oil
1 C	Lemon juice
1 tsp	Garlic salt
1 tsp	Dry mustard
1 tsp	Beau Monde
1	Egg

METHOD

1. Toss the first 6 ingredients in large bowl.

2. Measure oil, lemon juice, spices and egg in a small bowl. Beat with a wire whisk until well combined and creamy. Pour evenly over salad, toss lightly.

3. Spoon into avocado halves, letting the salad spill over the sides.

4. (For large groups, like a church supper, I double the recipe, chop the avocados and add them to the salad).

Everyday Salad

From Claire Bennett*

INGREDIENTS

1	head lettuce
12	grape tomatoes
3	ribs celery
1	red onion
1	cucumber
1	can black beans, rinsed and drained
1 pkg	sliced almonds, plain or seasoned
1 pkg	crumbled goat cheese or Feta
¼ C	Craisins

METHOD

1. Tear the fresh lettuce into bite-sized pieces (tearing avoids brown edges). Put in big bowl.

2. Cut the grape tomatoes in half, chop the celery and add to the lettuce.

3. Thinly slice as much red onion as desired, then separate the pieces.

4. Peel and quarter the cucumber. Remove the seeds, then chop into ½ inch pieces.

5. Add the rinsed and drained black beans, almonds, cheese, and Craisins.

6. Toss and dress. I always set several bottles of dressing on the table and let everyone choose their favorite.

*Claire is renowned in Chapel Springs for her lack of culinary expertise. It maxed out at Jell-O. But she can make a mean salad.

Great Aunt Lola's Taco Salad

4 servings

INGREDIENTS

1 lb	ground beef
1 pkg	taco seasoning
1	head of lettuce, shredded
1	avocado, diced
1	large tomato, diced
1	can pinto beans, drained
1 8 oz	package of shredded Mexican cheese or cheddar
1	package of tortilla chips, broken up
1	bottle of Catalina (or French) dressing

METHOD

1. Fry the ground beef until browned. Add the taco seasoning (depending on your family's taste, use ½ to the whole package). Cool to room temperature.

2. Mix the lettuce, avocado, tomato, and beans in a large bowl. Then add the meat and cheese. Mix well. Then add the dressing and just before serving, toss in half the chips. Serve the remaining as a side.

SOUPS

Beef Vegetable Soup

From Olympia Gordon*

Serves 8

INGREDIENTS

3-4	cross-cut beef shanks
4 Tbsp	olive oil
1	onion, diced
3-4	carrots
2-3	ribs celery
	Water
3	bay leaves
	Egg noodles or rice
½ lb	fresh green beans, cleaned and trimmed
2 Tbsp	(heaping) beef base (I use Better Than Bullion brand), dissolved in a cup of warm water.
	Salt, pepper, and garlic powder to taste
	Add any other vegetables you like

METHOD

1. In an 8-10 quart soup pot, lightly caramelize the onions in 2 Tbsp of the olive oil. Set aside.

2. Add the remaining olive oil and brown the beef shanks. When they have a good sear on them, add the onions and the other vegetables. Add the beef base and enough water to fill the pot to within

2 inches of the top. Add salt, pepper, and garlic powder to taste.

3. Cook uncovered and reduce; until losing 3 inches of liquid, and the meat falls off the bone. Break up the meat and add noodles or rice as desired. Check seasoning and add more if needed. Discard bones and bay leaves before serving.

*Olympia's hubby, Lester, loves this soup. And Olympia chased Lester around the block with a cast iron skillet because he took the entire pot to the Post Office to share with his coworkers. The only problem was Olympia had made it for the church potluck the next night.

Butternut Squash Soup

From Vicky Adams, Vicky owns *Déjà vu**

INGREDIENTS

I	Butternut squash, cut in 2, seeds removed.
	olive oil
3 Tbsp	butter
I	med onion
I Tbsp	freshly grated ginger
3 C	chicken stock
	salt & white pepper to taste

METHOD

1. Brush sheet pan w/olive oil. Roast squash (flesh side down) at 350, 45 minutes. Remove from oven and cool.

2. Melt butter and sauté onion and ginger for about 5 minutes. Add chicken stock and simmer about 10 minutes, covered.

3. When squash is cooled, scoop out flesh. Add to stock/onion mixture and use a stick blender to mix.

4. Add salt and white pepper. (If it's too thick, add a little water.)

*Vicky hasn't made her debut yet, but will in *Home to Chapel Springs,* coming in May, 2016

Slow-cooker Potato Soup

From Cooper Benson

INGREDIENTS

I	bag (32 oz) frozen southern-style diced hash brown potatoes, thawed
½ C	chopped onion
I	medium stalk celery, diced (1/2 cup)
I	carton (32-oz) chicken broth
I C	water
3 Tbsp	all-purpose flour
I C	milk
I	bag (8 oz) shredded cheese blend (2 cups)
¼ C	real bacon pieces
4 (or ¼ C) medium green onions, sliced	

METHOD

1. In a slow cooker, mix potatoes, onion, celery, broth and water. Cover; cook on low heat setting 6 to 8 hours.

2. In small bowl, mix flour into milk; stir into potato mixture. Increase heat setting to high. Cover; cook 20 to 30 minutes or until mixture thickens.

3. Stir in cheese until melted. Garnish individual servings with bacon bits.

Salmon Soup

From Miss Cora Lee Rice*

Get yourself bubbling with this savory soup. Just add some homemade bread and butter and watch your brood gobble it up. Mine can't get enough!

INGREDIENTS

3 Tbls	butter
¾ C	chopped onion
½ C	chopped celery
1 tsp	garlic powder
2 C	diced potatoes
2	carrots, diced
2 C	chicken broth
1 tsp	salt
1 tsp	pepper
1 tsp	dill
2 (16 oz)	cans salmon or boil 1 lb of salmon filet (fresh or frozen) in water and use some of the fish water to add to the soup)
1	can evaporated milk (or 1 can of goat's milk)
1	can creamed corn
½ lb	cheddar cheese, shredded

METHOD

1. Melt the butter and sauté the onion, celery, and garlic powder. Stir in the potatoes, carrots, broth, salt, pepper, and dill.

2. Bring to a boil, then reduce to a simmer for 20 minutes. Stir in chopped salmon, milk, corn and add cheese. (If you boiled fresh or frozen salmon, add in some of the water as desired).

3. Serve with crusty bread.

*Miss Cora Lee was Carin Jardine's grandmother. You'll meet Carin in *Home to Chapel Springs*, coming to you in May, 2016.

MAIN COURSE

BBQ Casserole

From Patsy Kowalski, Artist and Claire's gallery
partner*

INGREDIENTS

I lb	ground beef
½ lb	sausage
¼ C	mustard
3 Tbsp	Brown sugar
I	can pork and beans
I	can tomato sauce
I	can biscuits

METHOD

1. Cook meats together until brown. Drain well. Add
    other ingredients except biscuits. Pour mixture into
    greased baking dish. Cut each biscuit into fourths
    and place on top of mixture.

2. Bake at 350° for 15 minutes or until biscuits are
    brown.

*This recipe is simple but delicious. Claire and I served it
to our kiddos when they were young. Either her 5 were at
my house or my 3 were at hers. Either way, we had a lot of
mouths to feed, and this recipe filled everyone up just fine.

Caldo Verde

From Olympia Gordon, who works at the Spa*

INGREDIENTS

3-4	links Italian sweet sausage
I	32 oz container chicken broth
3	large potatoes, chopped into bite sized chunks
I lb	kale

METHOD

1. Heat stockpot on medium heat. Cut sausage into 1/2 –inch pieces and cook 4-5 minutes or until golden brown. Add broth and chopped potatoes. Reduce heat to med-low and cook for 18-20 minutes, until potatoes begin to soften.

2. Stir in kale, cook 10-12 minutes until potatoes and kale are tender.

*Olympia chased her husband, Lester (Chapel Springs Postmaster), down the street with a frying pan after he ate most of the Caldo Verse she'd prepared for when her family was visiting. They were left with nothing to eat but canned chili.

Elephant Stew

From Mayor Felix Riley's Mama
Mayor Riley says: My mama will kill me for sharing
this. Serves: 3,500

INGREDIENTS

I	medium elephant
2	(50 gallon) containers broth
500 lbs	assorted fresh vegetables, chopped
I00 lbs	tomatoes, peeled and chopped
½	ton potatoes, peeled and chopped
2	rabbits (optional)

METHOD

1. Cut elephant into bite-size pieces. This will take about 2 months.

2. Using large kettles, simmer equal parts elephant and vegetables with enough broth to cover. Cook for a couple days.

3. If more are expected, add the rabbits. But do this only if necessary since most people don't like to find hare in their stew.

Felix's Classic Firehouse Chili

From Mayor Felix Riley

Mayor Riley says: My brother swears, though it nearly kills him to do so, this is the best chili he's ever had. I'm not so modest. This *is* the best chili, hands down. That's why I win (or should win) the chili contest every year.

INGREDIENTS

2 Tbls	olive oil
1 lb	lean ground beef
1 lb	ground pork (not pork sausage, although that could work too)
1 lb	bacon
1	large onion, chopped
1	red bell pepper, chopped
6	cloves garlic, minced
2 15-ounce	cans diced tomatoes (I use the preseasoned kind, but don't tell)
1 C	double-brewed, dark coffee (use twice the coffee you normally would)
1	bottle dark beer (don't fret, the alcohol burns off)
1	can kidney beans, drained and rinsed
1	can cannellini beans, drained and rinsed
1	can black beans, drained and rinsed
½ tsp	ground cayenne pepper, or to taste
2-3 Tbls	brown sugar (depending upon taste, I use 3)
1½ tsp	dried oregano

	Salt and pepper to taste
2 Tbls	ground cumin
¼ C	chili powder (I've been known to add a smidge more)
	Liquid smoke to taste (optional)

METHOD

1. I hate clean up, so I try to do as much in one pan as I can. In a large slow cooker with the ability to brown meat, heat olive oil on brown (if your stockpot has that setting). Add onions and cook 2-3 minutes. Add red peppers and garlic and cook another 2-3 minutes. Add ground beef and ground pork and cook until meat is browned. (Of course, you can fry it all in a skillet, too, and add in separately, but why?)

2. Fry and crumble the bacon. (I like to oven fry. Less mess.) Add crumbled bacon to slow cooker.

3. Next, add all other ingredients. Stir to combine. Taste and adjust seasoning, adding additional salt, pepper, oregano, cumin, or chili powder to taste. Set slow cooker on low and cook 8-10 hours. No peeking! Taste, and adjust seasoning. Invite all your friends and be prepared to be fawned over.

Hannah's Pork Lung

From Hannah Tucker

(No lungs involved, but this got its name from a brother-in-law when his mother-in-law tried to recreate on her own, and well...it looked interesting)

INGREDIENTS

> Pork or Chuck roast (or even a venison roast)
> Mix ¼ C mustard and ¼ C BBQ sauce
> Coat roast with mixture.

METHOD

1. Bake in oven at 375° until done (about 1 hr)

2. Hannah made this up when she was 13 and was handed a deer or calf roast and asked to cook it.

Shepherd's Pie

From Kelly Appling, owner of *The Gifted Gifter*
She is also the artistic director of Lakeside Players

Serves 4-6 but can be expanded easily

INGREDIENTS

I lb	Ground beef
I	small onion (or ½ large one), diced
	olive oil
I – 4	cloves of garlic (this depends on how much you like garlic. I don't think one can ever have too much)
I (14 oz)	can of corn, drained
I (14 oz)	can of diced tomatoes, drained
3 – 4	potatoes, cooked and mashed

METHOD

1. Brown the onion and garlic in some olive oil. When it's slightly caramelized add the ground beef and cook till brown. Add the corn and tomatoes, and cook for 5 minutes. Drain off grease.

2. Put the meat mixture in a baking dish, top with the mashed potatoes and bake for 20-25 minutes at 350°

3. This is an old family staple, a one-dish meal. It's also cheap. Serve it with bread rolls. It's the kind of thing you simply throw together. I guessed at the amounts. You can adjust them to your tastes. You can add other things if you want, like mushrooms or peas.

Southern-fried Chicken

From Great Aunt Lola*

INGREDIENTS

I	Chicken cut in pieces (legs, thighs, wings & breasts)
3 C	Buttermilk
I	Egg, beaten
I C	Milk
2 C	Flour
2 Tbls	Salt
2 Tbls	Pepper
2 Tbls	Garlic powder
2 tsp	Onion powder
2 Tbls	paprika
	Peanut oil to fry chicken

METHOD

1. Soak the chicken pieces in buttermilk overnight. Discard the buttermilk.

2. Beat the egg with the milk and put it in a bowl. Mix seasonings, salt & pepper with the flour and divide into 2 bowls.

3. Dredge chicken pieces in the seasoned flour, then in the egg mixture, then in the second bowl of flour.

4. Fill your cast iron skillet (What? You don't have a cast iron skillet? Honey, you need one for Southern fried chicken!) about 1/3 of the way up with Peanut oil.

5. When the oil reaches 350°, place the chicken in the skillet. Cook, turning a couple of times, until golden brown and the internal temperature registers 165° F, approximately 15 minutes.

*Yes, Great Aunt Lola could cook up a storm. It's how she caught all those husbands.

Spaghetti Pie

From Patsy Kowalski

INGREDIENTS

1 lb	ground beef
½ lb	pork sausage
1	large jar spaghetti sauce
1 lb	angel hair pasta
2 Tbsp	butter
¼ - ½ C	Parmesan cheese
1 tsp	basil
2	beaten eggs
16 oz	cottage cheese
1 pkg	shredded mozzarella cheese

METHOD

1. Brown the ground beef and pork sausage. Drain well. Stir in the spaghetti sauce. Cook and drain the pasta per package instructions.

2. Mix the butter, Parmesan cheese, basil, and eggs. Toss with angel hair pasta. Pour noodles in a greased 9x13 baking dish.

3. Spread the cottage cheese over noodles, then layer sauce mixture on top of cheese. Sprinkle with mozzarella. Cover and bake at 350° for 30 minutes.

4. This is another recipe from Claire's and my youth. Mama taught us to make it when we were 10

years old. Claire's failed miserably, poor thing. She never could get the idea of measuring or following directions. But she makes the most beautiful bowls and platters to serve food in.

Stuffed Mirlitons (Vegetable Pear)

From Cooper Benson, Patsy Kowalski's mother and a famous artist

24 servings

INGREDIENTS

12	large mirlitons
4/5 C	celery, chopped
1 ½ C	diced onion
1	Bell pepper, diced fine
1 ½ C	seasoned breadcrumbs
3 C	cooked chopped shrimp (or sausage)
9 Tbsp	cooking oil
	Season to taste

METHOD

1. Cut the militons in half lengthwise. Remove any seeds. Boil until tender. Scoop out the meat, reserving the shell for stuffing. Mash the meat of the pears.

2. In a medium skillet, sauté onion, bell pepper, and celery until tender. Add the mashed mirlitons, cooked shrimp (or sausage), 1 C of breadcrumbs,

and season to taste. Stuff the mixture into the shells. Top with ½ C breadcrumbs.

3. Place the stuffed mirlitons in a baking dish and heat in a 350° oven for 20 minutes or until breadcrumbs are brown.

4. I understand these can freeze quite nicely for up to 6 months.

Wasabi Salmon

From Patsy Kowalski

Serves 4

INGREDIENTS

1 Tbls	wasabi powder
1 tsp	Beau Monde
1 Tbls	water
1 C	bread crumbs
1 Tbls	rice wine vinegar
¼ C	Sesame oil
4 (6-oz)	salmon fillets, skinned
¼ tsp	soy sauce

Orange-Ginger Sauce, recipe follows

¼ C	toasted sesame seeds, garnish

METHOD

1. In a little bowl, stir 1 Tbls of water into the wasabi to make a paste. Whisk in vinegar and soy. Place salmon in a Pyrex baking dish. Coat both sides evenly with wasabi mixture. Season lightly with the Beau Monde.

2. Put bread crumbs in a shallow dish. Coat both sides of the fillets evenly in the crumbs. You can press the crumbs to make them adhere. Line a cookie sheet with wax paper. Lay the salmon on it and refrigerate for 30 minutes.

3. Heat sesame oil in a large skillet over medium-high

heat. Cook the fish until desired doneness, (medium-rare is best - 3 to 4 minutes per side depending on how thick the fillet). Plate the fish, drizzle with the Orange-Ginger Sauce, and dust with the seeds.

ORANGE-GINGER SAUCE:

INGREDIENTS

¼ C	minced shallots
½ C	heavy cream
1 Tbls	minced ginger
1 C	dry white wine
2 Tbls	orange zest
1 tsp	soy sauce
1 C	orange juice
1/8 tsp	wasabi powder
2	sticks cold unsalted butter, cut into pieces
	Salt

METHOD

1. In a saucepan, combine the first 5 ingredients and bring to a boil. Reduce the heat to medium-low. Reduce (by simmering) by 2/3. Add the cream and cook until reduced by half.

2. Whisking constantly, add the pieces of butter one at a time, waiting until each is completely melted before adding the next piece. Continue whisking until the sauce is smooth.

3. Add the soy, wasabi, and salt to taste. Makes about 1 cup. If not being served immediately, place in a hot water bath, covered, and stir occasionally.

SIDE DISHES

Beethoven's Beans

From Joel Bennett*

Serves 16-20

INGREDIENTS

2 16 oz	cans Baked Beans
1 32 oz	can Pork 'n' Beans
1 lb	Kielbasa
1 lb	ground beef
1 ½ C	Hickory smoked Bar-B-Q sauce
1 Tbls	Yellow mustard
2/3 C	Brown sugar
¼ C	Molasses
1	Medium onion chopped

METHOD

1. Over a medium heat, brown onion in some olive oil, add beef and Kielbasa. Cook until liquids are reabsorbed into the meat.

2. Drain juice off beans. When meat is done, add all ingredients together and mix well. Bake in a large baking pan, uncovered, at 350º for 1 hour (in a gas oven, cook at 400º for 1 hour)

3. Beans will be brown around the sides of the pan. This can be put together the day before and baked an hour before serving.

*Joel is the chef in the Bennett household, and that suits Claire, because husband-cooked anything is her favorite.

Pineapple Casserole

From Patsy Kowalski

INGREDIENTS

½ C	sugar
3 Tbsp	plain white flour
3 Tbsp	pineapple juice
1 C	shredded cheddar cheese
1 20 oz	can drained pineapple chunks
¾ C	crushed CHEEZ-IT crackers
¼ C	melted margarine

METHOD

1. Combine the sugar, flour and pineapple juice. Add the cheddar cheese and pineapple chunks. Spoon it into a greased 1 quart casserole dish.

2. Mix the CHEEZ-IT crackers and melted margarine, and sprinkle over top of pineapple mixture.

3. Bake at 350° for 20 to 30 minutes or until crumbs are golden brown.

Rice Casserole

From Great Aunt Lola

It's not low fat, and has a ton of butter, but oh, is it delicious!

Serves 6-8 as a side dish

INGREDIENTS

2 C	Uncle Ben's rice
2	cans beef consume
2	cans water
2	bullion cubes
2	cans sliced mushrooms
I tsp	marjoram
3 tsp	anise seed
I lb	butter, cut up

METHOD

1. Mix all ingredients together and let stand about 2 hours. Cover and bake @ 350°F for 1 hour. Stir after 30 or 40 minutes. If necessary, add more water.

Sweet Potatoes

From Cooper Benson*

INGREDIENTS

2	large cans of yams
2 C	mini marshmallows
I C	chopped pecans

METHOD

1. Mash the yams and put in casserole dish. Top with marshmallows and chopped pecans.

2. Bake at 325° until marshmallows are toasted brown and melting.

*Cooper wasn't a renowned cook but a renowned artist. She got by in the kitchen with easy but tasty dishes. However, that's why Patsy is such a great cook.

VEGETABLES

Baked Sugar Snap Peas

From Adrianna Bennett
Claire & Joel's eldest daughter*

INGREDIENTS

2 Tbsp   shallots, chopped
1 Tbsp   fresh thyme or basil, chopped
1 lb   sugar snap peas
1 Tbsp   olive oil
Optional: slivered almonds

METHOD

1. Preheat oven to 400°

2. Remove strings from pea pods.

3. Chop shallots and herbs.

4. Layer peas on a baking sheet with shallots and herbs, then drizzle with oil. Bake 8-10 minutes or until crisp and tender.

5. Sprinkle with salt and pepper to taste.

6. If desired, just before removing from oven, top with slivered almonds.

*Adrianna moved to Nashville and applied her computer science degree to the music industry. She called her daddy to get this recipe for a taste of home. It's her favorite snack.

Crispy Green Bean "Fries"

From Lydia Smith-Sanders*

This is a delicious and healthy alternative to French fries

INGREDIENTS

I lb	fresh green beans, washed and trimmed
3 Tbsp	olive oil
½ C	grated Parmesan cheese
I tsp	kosher salt
I tsp	freshly ground pepper
½ tsp	paprika (for a smoky taste, use smoked paprika)

METHOD

1. Preheat oven to 375°.

2. Line a baking sheet with parchment paper.

3. In a large bowl, toss the green beans with olive oil. Add Parmesan cheese, salt, pepper, and paprika. Toss well to coat.

4. Pour the green beans onto the parchment lined baking sheet and bake until crisp, about 10 to 15 minutes.

5. Cool slightly before serving.

*You met Lydia in *Chapel Springs Revival*. In *Chapel Springs Survival*, she is now Lydia Sanders. The widow on the hill became a blushing bride.

Sautéed Spinach and Portobellos

From Esther Tully, Owner of *Leave the World Behind* Bookstore

INGREDIENTS

8 oz	baby Portobello mushrooms, sliced or quartered
1	9 oz. bag of fresh spinach
3 Tbsp	garlic herb butter (homemade – recipe below or store bought)
¼ tsp	salt
¼ tsp	pepper
¼ C	Parmesan cheese

HERB GARLIC BUTTER

INGREDIENTS

1 C	butter
2 Tbsp	chopped fresh herbs (basil, dill, rosemary, and parsley)
1	minced garlic clove
1 tsp	olive oil

METHOD

1. Place the garlic, herbs, and butter in a large bowl. Start mixer on slow, increasing speed as you cream the butter and herbs. Add olive oil.

2. Melt herb butter in large sauté pan over med heat. Cook mushrooms, salt, and pepper 2-3 minutes or until mushrooms are tender. Add spinach, cover, and cook until wilted (2-3 minutes).

3. Reduce heat to low, and simmer 3-4 minutes. Stir in Parmesan cheese.

HOLIDAYS

Cornbread Dressing

From Eileen Carlson*

INGREDIENTS FOR CORNBREAD

1 cup	self-rising cornmeal
3/4 cup	buttermilk
2	eggs
2 Tbls	vegetable oil

DRESSING

	cornbread, crumbled
8 Tbls	butter (1 stick)
2 C	celery, chopped
1	large onion, chopped
4 C	chicken stock
1 tsp	salt
1 tsp	black pepper
1 tsp	sage (optional)
1	10 ½ oz can cream of chicken soup
1 Tbls	poultry seasoning (optional)

METHOD

1. For cornbread: Preheat oven to 350.

2. Combine all ingredients and mix well. Pour batter into a greased shallow baking dish. Bake for approximately 20 to 25 minutes.

3. Remove from oven and let cool.

For Dressing:.

1. Preheat oven to 350.

2. Melt the butter in a large skillet over medium heat. Add the celery and onion and cook until transparent, approximately 5 to 10 minutes.

3. Pour the vegetable mixture over cornbread mixture. Add the stock and mix well. Add salt, pepper, sage and poultry seasoning to taste. Pour mixture into a greased baking dish and bake until dressing is cooked through, about 45 minutes.

*The mayor loves this one. He can't get enough.

Jalapeño Dressing

From Eileen Carlson

INGREDIENTS

1	Onion, chopped
2	ribs Celery, chopped
1	can Faro jalapeños (mild, drained)
2	boxes Stove Top boxed corn bread stuffing mix
3	hard-boiled eggs, chopped
3 C	chicken broth
1	chicken bullion cube
8 oz	sour cream
1	can of cream of chicken soup
1	can cream of mushroom soup
1 tsp	sage
1 tsp	poultry seasoning
1 tsp	garlic powder
	Salt and Pepper to taste
	Butter

METHOD

1. Sauté onion and celery in 1 stick of butter. Add Faro canned jalapeños (mild, drained), 1 bullion cube, 3 cups chicken broth and bring to a boil.

Add 2 boxes cornbread stuffing mix, cover with lid. Turn off heat and let sit for 5 minutes.

2. In a separate container, mix 3 hard boiled eggs (chopped), 1 can cream of mushroom soup, 1 can cream of chicken, sour cream, sage, poultry seasoning, garlic powder, salt and pepper to taste.

3. Add second mixture to first mixture, stir well. Pour into a baking dish and bake at 325 for 45 minutes.

Optional:
1. Add chicken or turkey.

2. Eggplant: 2 boiled, peeled, mashed, drained eggplant and 1 pound ground meat.

3. Squash: 1 to 2 bags frozen squash, mashed boiled, add crumbled Ritz crackers to top the baking dish.

Sausage & Oyster Stuffing

from Joel Bennett

INGREDIENTS

1-2	packages of seasoned stuffing mix (I prefer Pepperidge Farm)
8 oz	butter (1 stick)
1	8 oz pkg sausage links (you'll use the grease and the meat from 4 links)
2 C	diced onions
1-2 Tbls	minced garlic
2-3	celery ribs, diced (dice some of the leaves)
1 C	mushrooms, chopped
1	8 oz can whole oysters, chopped and reserve liquid
1 tsp	sage
1 32 oz	container of chicken stock
	salt and pepper to taste

METHOD

1. Preheat the oven to 350° F.

2. Dice all the vegetables. In a large skillet, cook the 4 sausage links. When done, remove the sausage and set aside. When cool, chop into pieces.

3. In the same skillet, caramelize the onion and garlic. Add the celery and mushrooms, and sauté until the celery is clear. Add the chopped sausage and

oysters. Stir to blend. Add salt, pepper, and sage to taste.

4. In a large bowl, combine stuffing mix, and vegetable mixture, tossing to mix well. Add the reserved oyster liquid and enough chicken broth* to make the dressing hold together.

5. Put dressing in a covered casserole dish and bake at 350° F for 45 minutes.

*If you are going to stuff a turkey to roast, use less liquid as it will absorb liquid from the bird. Refrigerate until cold before stuffing the turkey.

Sweet Potatoes in Orange Halves

Wonderful for Thanksgiving or Christmas
From Joel Bennett

Serves 8

INGREDIENTS

7	large sweet potatoes, about 3 lbs
4	large oranges, halved
1	stick unsalted butter
1/2 cup	light brown sugar
3	large eggs
3/4 cup	fresh orange juice
1/2 cup	heavy cream
1/4 cup	brandy*
1 tsp	ground cinnamon
1/2 tsp	ground nutmeg
1/2 tsp	salt

METHOD

1. Bake potatoes at 400° until tender (about 1 hour). Remove from the oven and let rest until cool enough to handle. Reduce oven temp to 350° F.

2. Scoop out the pulp from the orange halves, leaving only the shell. Set the shells aside to be filled later.

3. While still warm, either peel the potatoes or scoop out the pulp and place it in a large bowl. Toss the

skins and stringy fibers. Add butter and beat out lumps with an electric mixer. Add sugar, eggs, orange juice, heavy cream, and brandy, and mix until smooth. Finally, add the cinnamon, nutmeg, and salt. Mix well, and add more seasoning if needed.

4. Spoon the sweet potato mixture into the orange halves, rounding off and smoothing the top. Bake until puffed and slightly golden, about 20 minutes.

*If you're a Southern Baptist or a teetotaler, you can skip the brandy. Pastor Seth doesn't touch the stuff, but when he learned that the alcohol baked out, and he could safely indulge in these delectable sweet taters, he became Joel's biggest fan.

Southern-fried Turkey

From Joel Bennett

Be sure y'all set the turkey fryer out on the cement. Don't try this on your wooden deck. Follow the turkey fryer manufacturer's directions. Do this the proper way, and you'll love it.

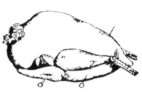

First thing to do is brine the bird. Brining alters the structure of the muscles, allowing it to absorb more moisture and flavor, resulting in a juicy bird.

INGREDIENTS

Brine:

¾ C   salt
¾ C   sugar
I C   hot water
¾   gallon cold water

Seasoning:

I   Tony Chachere's Cajun Seasoning
Garlic butter, melted
Turkey injector to inject the garlic butter
Peanut oil for frying

METHOD

1. **To brine the turkey**: Mix the salt and sugar in 1 cup of hot water. Stir to dissolve. Add the ¾ gallon of cold water. Put in the **thawed** turkey with the giblets removed. Use a plate to weigh the turkey down and refrigerate for 24 hours. The next day,

remove the bird from the brine, rinse and pat the dry.

Prepare the bird for frying:

1. Using an injector, inject **melted garlic butter** into the bird, going deep into the meat. (I use Publix. If you aren't blessed to live in the South, see if your grocery store makes garlic butter or garlic spread and use that).

2. Next, season the bird. The best way is use **Tony Chachere's Cajun Seasoning**. Be liberal, coating the bird well, inside and out.

3. Fill the fryer with **Peanut Oil** to the indicated level. Don't you be a turkey and think you need more. Follow the manufacturer's directions.

To cook the turkey:

1. Approximately 90 minutes before calling the hoards to feast, heat the oil to the manufacturer's recommended temperature. When the oil is ready, CAREFULLY lower the bird in, then cover. Deep-fry that baby for 3 minutes per pound or as the manufacturer recommends.

2. When done, CAREFULLY remove the bird and let rest for a half hour. Then carve and enjoy. You'll never go back to roasted turkey again.

Six-layer Eggnog Cake

Author

INGREDIENTS

2 C	all-purpose flour
2 tsp	double-acting baking powder
½ tsp	nutmeg
½ tsp	salt
1 ½ C	heavy cream
½ tsp	rum extract
4	eggs
1 ¼ C	Sugar
4	squares semi-sweet chocolate
	red and green food coloring
2-3	cans of buttery chocolate frosting

METHOD

1. At least 4 hours ahead of serving or a day ahead: Preheat oven to 350ºF. Grease and flour three 9" round cake pans. You can put a circle of wax paper in the bottom, if desired.

2. In a small bowl, with a fork, combine flour, baking powder, nutmeg and salt; set aside. In another small bowl with mixer at medium speed, beat heavy cream and rum extract until stiff peaks form.

3. In a large bowl using the same beaters, with mixer at high speed, beat eggs and sugar until thick and

lemon colored, about 5 minutes. With a wire whisk or rubber spatula, gently fold in the flour mixture and whipped cream into egg mixture until blended; pour batter into cake pans.

4. In 2 of the cake pans, add a few drops of red and green food coloring and gently blend. Stagger pans on 2 oven racks so no pan is directly over another. Bake 20 to 25 minutes until a toothpick inserted in the center comes out clean.

5. Cool on wire racks 10 minutes; remove from pans and cool completely, about 1 hour. Meanwhile, make chocolate curls for garnish. Using the heat of your hands or in a slightly warm oven, slightly soften chocolate squares. With a vegetable peeler, shave chocolate into curls and set aside.

6. When the cake layers are completely cool, with a sharp knife, cut each cake layer horizontally in half. I use toothpicks around the circumference of the cake layer to mark where to cut. Place first layer on cake plate, cut side up; spread with a thin layer of frosting. Set the second layer on, cut side down. Repeat until all layers are stacked on top. Make sure the last layer is top-side up. Frost with remaining frosting. Garnish with chocolate curls. Refrigerate until serving time.

DESSERTS

Apple Dessert

from Hannah Tucker

INGREDIENTS

Apples

Snickers candy bars

METHOD

1. Slice apples real thin and place in bottom of a baking dish.

2. Chop up Snickers and place over apples .

3. Bake at 350 for about 15 minutes.

4. Really good fresh out of the oven and served with ice cream.

Banana Pudding

From Hannah Tucker

INGREDIENTS

3/4 cup	granulated sugar
1/3 cup	all purpose flour
	Dash of salt
2 cups	Carnation's evaporated milk
1/2 tsp	vanilla flavoring
35-45	vanilla wafers
5-6	med sized fully ripened bananas sliced
4	eggs separated at room temperature

METHOD

1. Combine 1/2 cup of the sugar, with the flour and salt, in top of double boiler (could see Claire trying to figure that out) stir in 4 egg yolks (reserving the whites) and the milk, blend well. Cook over boiling water, stirring constantly until thickened. Reduce heat and cook stirring occasionally for 5 minutes. Remove from heat and add vanilla.

2. Place a small amount on bottom of 1 1/2 quart dish(oven proof) cover with layer of wafers, bananas and custard, continue layering ending with custard.

3. Beat reserved egg whites until stiff and gradually add in the remaining 1/4 cup sugar. Beat until stiff

peaks form. Spoon on top of pudding and spread to cover entire top of pudding. Bake at 425 for 5 minutes or until lightly browned. Makes 8 servings

4. That's word for word minus the () phrases of my family cookbook banana pudding recipe...

Cherry Pie in a Cloud

From Kelly Appling

INGREDIENTS

1	refrigerated pie shell, baked. (Try Pillsbury All-Ready Pie Crusts)
1	Large Can (21 oz) Cherry Pie Filling
2 Tbsp	of Granulated sugar
1 ½ tsp	almond extract
16 oz.	(2-8 oz blocks) Cream Cheese, softened at room temp for 30 min.
1 ½ cups	Powdered sugar
1 Tbsp	Lemon Juice (bottled is fine)
1 tsp	Vanilla Extract
1 tsp	Almond Extract
⅔	of a 9-10 oz container of Cool Whip
⅓ C	Slivered or Sliced, Honey Roasted Almonds (optional - I use Sunkist)
	Maraschino Cherries, drained (optional final topping)

METHOD

1. Allow pie shell to come to room temperature, according to package directions. Unroll dough and spread in pie pan. Crimp the edges. Sprinkle unbaked pie shell lightly with about 1 Tbsp of granulated sugar. Prick holes generously in shell using a fork. Bake as directed on package until lightly golden brown. Allow to cool thoroughly.

2. Mix cream cheese, powdered sugar, lemon juice and vanilla in mixer at high speed until smooth and creamy. Use the mixer to gently fold in the Cool Whip until just blended in. Spread cream cheese mixture about ½" thick on bottom and up the sides of cooled pie shell. Make sure you create a well to put the cherry filling in. Reserve extra cream cheese filling for decoration.

3. Dump cherry pie filling into a bowl. Mix in almond flavoring and sugar. Add cherry filling to center of cream cheese-lined pie crust. If desired, use a large icing bag or electric cookie shooter with a decorative tip and pipe rosettes around the edge with some of the cream cheese mixture. Or just put rounded spoonsful of cream cheese mixture round the edge, overlapping the filling. Refrigerate until ready to serve.

4. If you want, sprinkle a few toasted, slivered almonds on top for an extra touch of flavor and crunch.

NOTE: Refrigerate leftovers, if there are any. This pie is great to make ahead and freeze. I make 2 and freeze 1. Just sit the pie out about an hour before serving. I leave it in the glass pie pan and wrap it in 3 layers of heavy-duty aluminum foil.

Coconut Cookies

From Grace Duval*

INGREDIENTS

½ C	butter
½ C	white sugar
1 tsp	vanilla
½ tsp	baking powder
2 C	plain corn flakes
½ C	brown sugar
1	egg
1¼ C	flour
½ tsp	salt
	small can coconut (1 1/3 C or 3 ½ oz)

METHOD

1. Cream together the butter, sugars, egg and vanilla. Add flour, baking powder, salt, baking soda, coconut, and corn flakes. Mix together thoroughly and chill.

2. Form into small balls and place on an ungreased cookie sheet. Bake at 350° for 10 - 20 minutes. Cool and remove to plate with a spatula.

*Grace Duval hasn't made her appearance yet. Keep an eye out for her.

Dee's Dough-less Peanut Butter Cookies

From Dee Lindstrom of Dee's 'n' Doughs

INGREDIENTS

1 C	sugar (I substitute 1 cup Splenda to make it Sugar-free)
1	large egg
1 C	creamy peanut butter
1 tsp	baking soda
½ tsp	vanilla

optional: 1/3 C chocolate chips

METHOD

1. In a large bowl, mix all ingredients. Roll level tablespoons into balls. Place on an ungreased baking sheet; flatten with a fork.

2. Bake at 350° for 18 minutes. Let cool slightly before removing from cookie sheet (they are a little fragile until cooled.)

3. **Yield:** 2 dozen.

4. Claire, did you know you can make this into a 3 ingredient cookie by using only the first 3 ingredients for an even quicker treat? The other ingredients just make it a little tastier.

5. And Trish I know you are going to ask. The recipe is correct. There is NO flour used in the making of this cookie.

Note: If you make sure your ingredients are Gluten-Free this can be a GF recipe. Some vanillas and all chocolate chips are not GF.

My Papa's Ugly Apple Cake

from Hannah Tucker

INGREDIENTS

2 C	sugar
2 C	all purpose flour
2 tsp	baking soda
2 tsp	salt
2 tsp	cinnamon
4 C	peeled and chopped apples
½ C	raisins
1 ½ C	salad oil (vegetable or olive oil works just fine, as I've made it with both since I didn't know what salad oil was)
2	eggs
2 tsp	vanilla

METHOD

1. Combine all ingredients in large bowl. Mix well.

2. Bake in 9x13 inch pan for 1½ hours at 325°

3. Add topping and return to oven and brown lightly....

TOPPING

¾ C	brown sugar	1 tsp	vanilla
2 tsp	water	½ C	shredded coconut
3 tsp	flour	1 C	chopped nuts (I've used walnuts and pecans)
3 tsp	butter melted		

Peanut Brittle

From Hannah Tucker

INGREDIENTS

2 C	sugar
½ C	karo light corn syrup
1/3 C	water
2 C	raw peanuts
2 tsp	butter
1 tsp	baking soda

METHOD

1. Mix first 3 ingredients and bring to boil. Add 2 cups raw peanuts (do not remove red hulls). When peanuts begin to pop, take off heat and immediately and add 2 tsp of butter and 1 tsp of baking soda. Stir.

2. Poor onto greased cookie sheet... cool... break into pieces and enjoy.

Grandma Riley's Southern Peach Cobbler

From Mayor Felix Riley's Grandma

Mayor Riley says, "When I eat this, and I eat it as often as I can, it makes me think of Grandma. That woman was a true southern chef. I don't want to get all sentimental, but when you make this you'll see what I mean."

INGREDIENTS

Filling:

5	pounds fresh peaches, peeled and sliced
1 ½ Tbls	fresh lemon juice
½ C	granulated sugar
2 Tbls	cornstarch
½ tsp	cinnamon

Topping:

2 C	all-purpose flour
6 Tbls	brown sugar
3 Tbls	granulated sugar, divided
½ tsp	salt
1 ½ tsp	baking powder
½ tsp	baking soda
2/3 C	sour cream
10 Tbls	butter, cut into 1/2" slices

METHOD

1. Preheat the oven to 425 F. Place the peaches in a large mixing bowl and sprinkle with the lemon juice.

2. In a small bowl, whisk together sugar, cornstarch, and cinnamon. Toss dry ingredients with the peaches. Spread the mixture in a 10 x 15-inch baking dish. Bake for 10 minutes.

3. To make the topping: In a food processor, combine flour, brown sugar, 2 Tbls of granulated sugar, baking powder, baking soda and salt. Add butter and pulse to chop into pea-sized pieces. Add sour cream and pulse just until mixed.

4. Remove peaches from the oven and drop the topping by large spoonsful onto the hot filling. Sprinkle the remaining granulated sugar over the topping. Bake for 15 to 18 minutes, until the filling is bubbling and the topping is golden brown. Serve warm.

Acknowledgements

Many thanks to our gracious and talented contributors (in alphabetical order by first name):

Becky Thompson, BBQ Casserole, Spaghetti Pie, Wasabi Salmon, Cole Slaw, & Pineapple Casserole

Betty Lacey, Fruity Baked Oatmeal

Dee Stevens, Dee's Dough Nut Bites, Asparagus Tart, & Dee's Doughless Peanut Butter Cookies

Elizabeth Ludwig, Sausage & Oyster Stuffing

Leanna Suhoversnik, Corn & Spinach Salad and Easy Living Salad

Margie Houmes, Salmon Soup

Marty Snowden, Coconut Cookies

Michael Ehret, Breakfast Casserole, Firehouse Chili, Southern Peach Cobbler

Michelle Morgan, Stuffed Mirlitons, Broccoli Salad, Potato Soup & Sweet Potatoes

Quita Chamberlain, Southwest Corn Salsa, Texas Caviar, Green Bean "Fries"

Tracy Lynn Roberts, Twisted Pretzel Biscuits, Pork Lung, Apple Dessert, Banana Pudding, Papa's Ugly Apple Cake, & Peanut Brittle

Chapel Springs Cookbook
sponsored by these fine books:

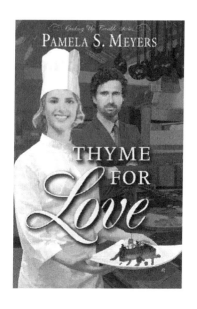

50453336R00061

Made in the USA
Charleston, SC
28 December 2015